1939

Nazi Germany invades Poland. Britain and France declare war on Germany and World War Two begins.

2nd September, 1945

Japan surrenders and World War Two ends.

1941

The US and the Soviet Union join the Allied forces.

7th December, 1941

Japanese forces launch a surprise attack on the US Pacific fleet at Pearl Harbour in Hawai'i.

7th May, 1945

Germany surrenders and the war in Europe is over.

Map of Charles Lindbergh's flight

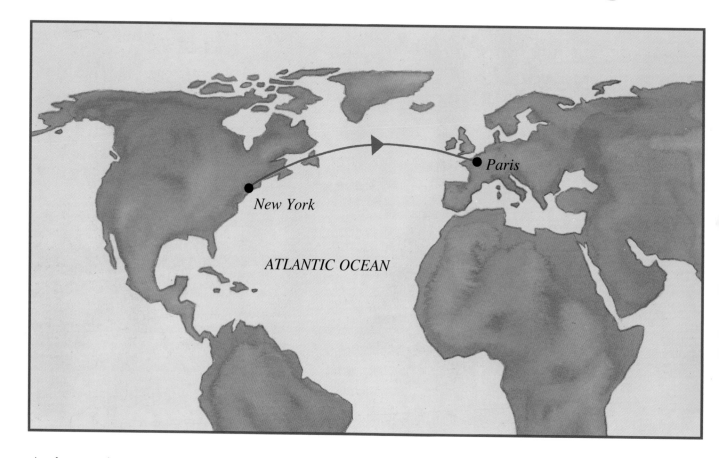

Aviator, inventor, explorer and author Charles Lindbergh made history in 1927 when he became the first person to fly across the Atlantic Ocean non-stop in his aircraft called Spirit of St. Louis. He was competing for the Orteig Prize – a reward offered to the first person to successfully complete the journey from New York city to Paris. Many other people were killed or injured in their attempts to win the prize before Lindbergh finally succeeded.

The amazing achievement made Lindbergh world-famous. He dedicated much of his time for years afterwards to promoting the possibility of commercial aviation and airmail.

Timeline

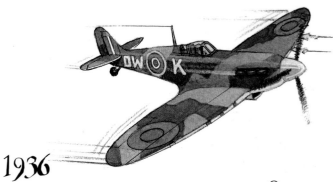

1933
The Nazi party come to power in Germany.

1936
The first flight of a Spitfire plane takes place.

1938
Spitfire planes begin to be manufactured in large numbers.

1937
R.J. Mitchell, designer of the Spitfire plane, dies at the age of 42.

1935
The first flight of a Messerschmitt Bf-109 takes place.

R.J. Mitchell

Author:
Ian Graham studied applied physics at the City University, London. He then took a postgraduate degree in journalism, specialising in science and technology. Since becoming a freelance author and journalist, he has written more than one hundred children's non-fiction books.

Artist:
David Antram was born in Brighton, England, in 1958. He studied at Eastbourne College of Art and then worked in advertising for fifteen years before becoming a full-time artist. He has illustrated many children's non-fiction books.

Series creator:
David Salariya was born in Dundee, Scotland. He has illustrated a wide range of books and has created and designed many new series for publishers in the UK and overseas. David established The Salariya Book Company in 1989. He lives in Brighton with his wife, illustrator Shirley Willis, and their son Jonathan.

Editor: **Jamie Pitman**

Editorial Assistant: **Mark Williams**

Published in Great Britain in MMXIX by
Book House, an imprint of
The Salariya Book Company Ltd
25 Marlborough Place, Brighton BN1 1UB
www.salariya.com

ISBN: 978-1-912537-31-0

SCRIBO BOOK HOUSE SCRIBBLERS

1 3 5 7 9 8 6 4 2

A CIP catalogue record for this book is available from the British Library.
Printed and bound in China.

Visit
www.salariya.com
for our online catalogue and
free fun stuff.

PAPER FROM
SUSTAINABLE
FORESTS

Don't worry, it's just a dent!

You Wouldn't Want to Be a World War Two Pilot!™

Written by
Ian Graham

Illustrated by
David Antram

Created and designed by
David Salariya

Air Battles You Might Not Survive

BOOK HOUSE
a SALARIYA *imprint*

Contents

Introduction

You are 16. Home is San Antonio in Texas, USA. The year is 1934. You're mad about aircraft and flying. There are model planes in your room and pictures of aircraft all over the walls. You go to your local airfield, Stinson Field, to watch the planes at every opportunity. Its name recently changed to Windburn Field, but everybody still calls it Stinson.

The pilots there tell you about Charles Lindbergh. He was the first person to fly across the Atlantic Ocean non-stop. Before he became world-famous, he did his military flight training in San Antonio and kept a plane of his own at Stinson Field.

Watching the planes veer left and right, you realise that flying a plane is very tricky, and that proper training is crucial to your skill and survival when you step in one. You may think it looks fun, but you've no idea what's in store for you in a few years' time!

> You call it hard work...I call it research!

YOU GET A JOB at the airfield cleaning the small private planes and helping the mechanics. You hang out with the pilots and talk to them about flying. One way or another, you're going to be a pilot too.

Learning to fly

You are sometimes paid for your work with flying time. Bit by bit, you get more time in the air with experienced pilots. You learn to fly and soon get your pilot's licence. Shortly after that, you take a job flying a crop-spraying plane on local farms.

Within a couple of years, you scrape together enough money to buy an old biplane of your own. When you get the chance, you fly at air fairs. People flock to see the aircraft and the flying displays the pilots put on. A favourite with the crowds is wing-walking. While you fly your plane, a friend stands on the top wing and waves to everyone. Spectacular as it is, it's a very risky business.

Flying solo

EVERY STUDENT PILOT has to make a successful flight alone before being awarded a pilot's licence. It's called 'going solo'. You go solo a week after your seventeenth birthday.

I'm a true fly boy* now!

*slang for 'pilot'

Air shows

Aaaarggh!

STUNT FLYING at air fairs in fragile 1930s planes can be very dangerous. A pilot can find himself hurtling towards the ground if a stunt goes wrong.

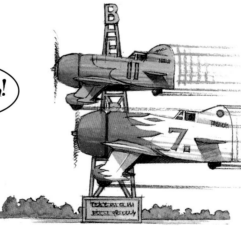

AIR RACES are popular in the 1930s. Crowds of spectators watch the planes racing each other. They fly around a course marked by towers called pylons.

YOU GIVE FLYING LESSONS and take people on sightseeing flights to help pay for your plane. People are very eager to get a taste of flying.

10

Squawk!
Handy hint
Remember to fasten your safety harness!
Looks like someone couldn't wait until lunchtime!
BRRRRRRRRRR!

Joining up

In the 1930s, the newspapers are full of stories about the coming war in Europe. In 1933, Adolf Hitler's sinister Nazi party comes to power in Germany. Then in 1939, Nazi Germany invades Poland. As a result, Britain and France declare war on Germany. World War II, the long, bitter war between the Axis powers and the Allied forces,* has begun.

You learn that the British Royal Air Force (RAF) is recruiting American pilots. The thought of flying fantastic modern fighters like the Hurricane and Spitfire, whilst helping the British to fight the Nazis, is too tempting. You apply to join the RAF, eager to start your training.

*The Axis powers included Germany, Japan, Italy, and several other countries. Great Britain, France, and Poland were among the major Allied nations at the start of the war. In 1941, the US and the Soviet Union joined the Allies.

KA-BOOM!!!

THE RAF ISN'T LOOKING for just any old pilot. You have to be able to say yes to a list of requirements:
• Are you between 20 and 31?
• Do you have a pilot's licence?
• Do you have 300 flying hours?
• Do you have good eyesight?
You don't need a college education or any military experience. That's a relief!

Handy hint

Pay attention in class, or you'll never be a fighter pilot.

PILOTS HAVE TO LEARN Morse code. It's a way of sending messages as a stream of short bleeps (dots) and long bleeps (dashes). Each letter is made up of a different set of dots and dashes.

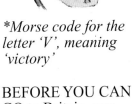

*Dot-dot-dot-dash**

Morse code for the letter 'V', meaning 'victory'

BEFORE YOU CAN GO to Britain, you must complete an RAF training course in the USA. You wave one last goodbye to your family and set off for the nearest training centre.

Sob!

Training

IT'S BEEN QUITE A WHILE since you were in school, and you struggle to keep up with some of the classes.

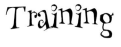

Piece of cake!

YOU DO YOUR FLIGHT TRAINING in a Stearman PT-17 biplane. It handles like your own biplane, so the lessons are easy. Most pilots go solo within 12 hours.

13

Language barrier

YOU CAN'T UNDERSTAND what your officers and mechanics are saying in their strange-sounding English accents.

Belt up!*

Are you a sprog,** old chum?

*Be quiet!

**a pilot fresh from training

YOUR TEXAN DRAWL sounds just like a foreign language to British ears.

Howdy y'all!

?

Fighter training

Xou arrive in Britain after a nerve-racking voyage across the Atlantic Ocean. As the passengers know very well, ships are at constant risk of attack by German submarines called U-boats. You begin to realise how much danger you are in. In London, you sign the official papers that make you an RAF officer and you are issued with your uniform.

Your next stop is an Operational Training Unit (OTU), where you will be trained to fly a fighter. You meet Polish pilots who have come to Britain to join the war effort too. The Poles form a Polish Air Force in Britain and its pilots fight courageously with the RAF.

Get stuck in!

THE SPITFIRE'S COCKPIT is so cramped that the pilot needs help to get strapped in. Mechanics help the pilot and then give the windscreen a final wipe before take-off.

GUNNERY PRACTICE involves firing your guns at a windsock, called a drogue, towed behind another plane.

RAT-A-TAT!

Leather helmet

Oxygen mask

Earphones

Lifejacket (called a 'Mae West' after a film star of the same name)

Leather gloves

Parachute

Sheepskin-lined boots

Handy hint

Keep an eye on your altitude!

Looking good, huh?

Censored

YOUR LETTERS HOME arrive with holes in them, because an official called a censor cuts out anything that he thinks might be useful to the enemy.

15

The Spitfire

R. J. Mitchell

THE SPITFIRE was designed by R. J. Mitchell, the leading British aircraft designer of the 1930s. Sadly, he never saw its success, because he died in 1937 at only 42 years of age.

Propeller

The Spitfire is the leading British fighter at the beginning of World War II. It's a small, fast and heavily armed plane. Its main job is to attack enemy aircraft, protecting Allied bombers from enemy fighters, and sometimes to strike at targets on the ground. The Spitfire proves to be such a good all-round aircraft that it is built in greater numbers than any other Allied fighter.

Whatta beauty!

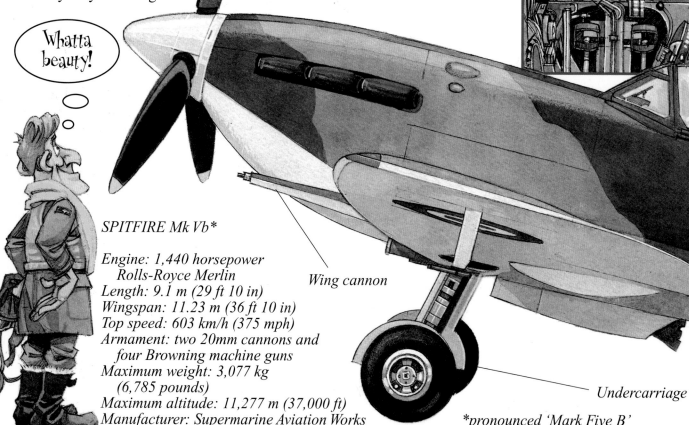

SPITFIRE Mk Vb*

Engine: 1,440 horsepower
Rolls-Royce Merlin
Length: 9.1 m (29 ft 10 in)
Wingspan: 11.23 m (36 ft 10 in)
Top speed: 603 km/h (375 mph)
Armament: two 20mm cannons and
four Browning machine guns
Maximum weight: 3,077 kg
(6,785 pounds)
Maximum altitude: 11,277 m (37,000 ft)
Manufacturer: Supermarine Aviation Works

Wing cannon

Undercarriage

*pronounced 'Mark Five B'

16

The Spitfire does not stay the same all through the war. There will be more than 20 different types of Spitfire with different wings, guns, engines and propellers. There is a navy version, too, called the Seafire.

Handy hint

Wear a silk scarf to keep your flying suit from rubbing your neck raw.

THE SPITFIRE'S COCKPIT (left) is just big enough for the pilot to squeeze in. The canopy (below) slides back to make more room for him to climb into the cockpit.

BELTS OF AMMUNITION are loaded into the guns from underneath the wings.

THE GROUND CREW swarms all over a Spitfire as soon as it lands. They refuel and re-arm it for the next mission.

Radio aerial

All-metal fuselage

Tail wheel

First posting

You arrive at an air base to join your fighter squadron. It's one of three RAF squadrons of American pilots, called Eagle Squadrons. You are replacing a young pilot just like yourself who was KIA.* It's yet another reminder of the dangers you face.

For every pilot, there are up to 10 men and women working on the ground to keep the planes repaired and ready for action. Each plane has its own crew chief and assistant. Together they look after the plane, giving work to other members of the ground crew if necessary.

WHEN YOU'RE ON cockpit alert, you have to sit in your plane for two hours, ready to go in case of an attack. If you see a bright flare bursting in the sky above you, you'd better scramble,** because enemy aircraft are about to arrive.

*Killed In Action
**take off as quickly as possible

SMALL SWASTIKAS (Nazi crosses) are sometimes painted on the side of a plane to show how many enemy aircraft the pilot has shot down. Each swastika represents one aircraft.

KAY

Wheeeeeeee!

There may be trouble ahead...

KA-POW!

Handy hint

A good landing is one you can walk away from.

Listen up! I'm only going to say this once…

Major Tom? Come in, Major Tom!

BEFORE EACH PLANNED MISSION, all the pilots who will take part attend a briefing to learn the details.

GROUND CONTROLLERS plot the positions of Allied planes and Axis planes on a map. They can hear the pilots and speak to them by radio.

19

Combat

It isn't long before you get your first taste of combat. It's exciting but the odds aren't great: a new fighter pilot in World War II has only a 50/50 chance of surviving his first five combat missions. Your first mission is to escort B-17 bombers on their journey to Germany. During the briefing, you begin to feel nervous. All the training is over and it's for real now. Lives will depend on what you do. The bombers have their own guns and gunners, but they can't manoeuvre quickly, making them easy targets for enemy fighters. You take off and join the bombers. On the way across the North Sea, you spot enemy fighters coming towards you!

Women at war

WHEN PLANES ARE LOST in combat, new planes are delivered by ferry pilots, many of whom are women.

PLANES OFTEN RETURN with battle damage. There might be bullet holes or part of a wing shot away. The ground crew have to repair the damage as fast as possible.

THE SOVIET UNION has regiments of women pilots. Pilots in the 588th Night Bomber Regiment are known as the Night Witches.

I hope this one lasts a bit longer!

The Night Witches fly old-fashioned Polikarpov Po-2 biplanes. They are slow, but they can turn quickly to escape an attack from an enemy fighter.

Allied and enemy fighters chase each other through the sky, twisting and turning to try to get enemy planes in their gunsights without leaving themselves exposed to enemy fire. Bursts of gunfire tear through the air.

The enemy fighters, out of ammunition, disappear as quickly as they arrived. You are relieved to have survived your first combat mission, but afterwards you realise how terrifying it was.

Handy hint

Keep looking around – enemy fighters can come from any direction.

Spitfire

B-17 bombers

Bandit* at two o'clock!

German FW-190 fighter

*enemy fighter

21

Passing time

Fighter pilots don't fly all day, every day, even in wartime. For some of the time, they are waiting on standby for the signal to dash to their planes and take off. As well as planned off-duty times, the weather may sometimes be too bad to fly, the airfield may be closed for repairs after an air raid, or planes might be out of service.

Pilots pass the time reading, writing letters home or playing games. They might be lucky enough to get weekend leave – permission to be off duty all weekend! Off-duty pilots in southern England head for London.

Zzz Zzz Zzz

Off duty in London

AMERICAN CITIES are brightly lit at night, but London and other British cities have to be kept dark. It's called the blackout. No-one is allowed to show any light at night, because it might guide enemy bomber pilots. People have to fit thick curtains to their windows at home to make sure that no light leaks outside. If any light gets out, you're in trouble!

Put that light out!

AIR-RAID PRECAUTIONS (ARP) wardens patrol the streets and make sure that no-one shows any light at night.

WATCHING A FILM or stage show is a favourite night out in London, but be prepared for it to be spoiled by an air raid.

THE WAILING SOUND of air-raid sirens warns everyone that enemy bombers are on the way and bombs will start falling soon.

LONDONERS SHELTER from the bombing in their own air-raid shelters, in public shelters, or in underground railway stations.

WHEN PEOPLE EMERGE from the shelters after an attack, some find that their homes are now just piles of rubble.

Bailing out

You wear a parachute, but it's not on your back. You sit on it! The parachute and a life raft double as a seat cushion. You hope you'll never need them.

One day, you are taken by surprise by a Messerschmitt Bf-109. The 109 is the leading German fighter and you're in its gunsights! As its pilot opens fire, bullets slam into the armour plate behind your head and shatter the cockpit canopy. Oil sprays out of bullet holes in your engine. You'll have to bail out!

YOU SLIDE THE SHATTERED CANOPY back and climb out of the cockpit into the cold air outside.

SHATTER!!

Aaaargh! I'm done for!

Messerschmitt Bf-109

RAT-A-TAT!!

AS YOU TUMBLE THROUGH THE AIR, you pull the ripcord handle and your parachute billows open above you.

Phew!

Handy hint

Remember how you were taught to roll when you land by parachute.

SPLISH!

Survival

IF YOU LAND IN THE SEA, your life raft will keep you afloat while you wait for a ship to pick you up.

I hope I don't get bounced...*

IF YOU HAVE TO WAIT to be picked up, or you land behind enemy lines, you may need your survival kit. It contains maps, money, a knife, matches and a compass.

*attacked by surprise

25

Pearl Harbor

On 7 December 1941, Japanese forces launch a surprise attack on the US Pacific fleet at Pearl Harbor, Hawai'i. More than 350 Japanese fighters, bombers and torpedo planes attack in two waves. Five midget submarines join the attack.

Americans, who have not suffered a major attack on their home territory in living memory, are shocked. The next day, the United States declares war on Japan. In return, Germany and Italy declare war on the United States. As a result, the United States decides to join the war in Europe as well as the war in the Pacific.

What's going on?

KA-BOOM!!

ZOOM!

Yesterday, December 7, 1941...

US PRESIDENT FRANKLIN D. ROOSEVELT gives one of the most famous speeches of the 20th century on the day after the attack.

SOME AMERICAN PILOTS in the RAF ask the US Embassy to transfer them to US forces. They get their wish, but not for another year.

AMERICAN FAMILIES hear their president describe the attack on the radio. The speech clearly marked America's intervention in the war.

Pacific fighters

Some of your friends became navy pilots and they are now fighting in the Pacific. Newspaper stories and newsreel films keep you up to date with their war. Navy pilots have to take off from, and land on, a heaving deck that looks the size of a postage stamp from the air. If they miss their ship, they're swimming home!

The most successful US navy fighter is the Grumman F6F-5 Hellcat. The leading Japanese navy fighter is the Mitsubishi A6M2. The Allies call it the Zero.

BOOM!

Japanese A6M2 Zero fighter

The fighters took off at precisely 0800* hours...

FILM REPORTS called newsreels are made throughout the war and shown in cinemas.

8am: pronounced 'oh-eight-hundred'

28

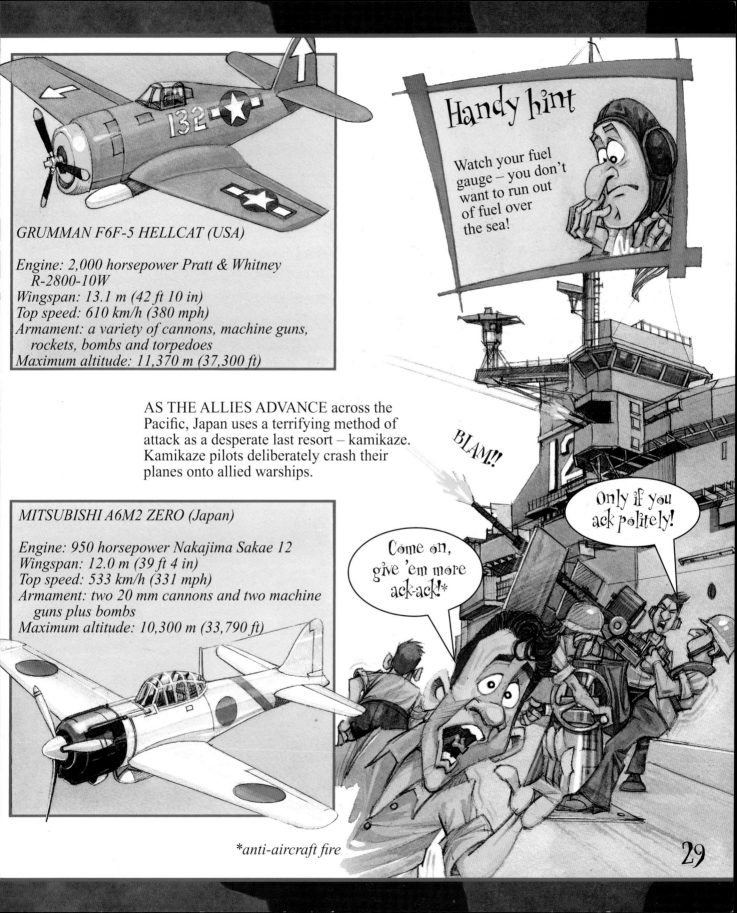

GRUMMAN F6F-5 HELLCAT (USA)

Engine: 2,000 horsepower Pratt & Whitney
R-2800-10W
Wingspan: 13.1 m (42 ft 10 in)
Top speed: 610 km/h (380 mph)
Armament: a variety of cannons, machine guns,
rockets, bombs and torpedoes
Maximum altitude: 11,370 m (37,300 ft)

AS THE ALLIES ADVANCE across the
Pacific, Japan uses a terrifying method of
attack as a desperate last resort – kamikaze.
Kamikaze pilots deliberately crash their
planes onto allied warships.

MITSUBISHI A6M2 ZERO (Japan)

Engine: 950 horsepower Nakajima Sakae 12
Wingspan: 12.0 m (39 ft 4 in)
Top speed: 533 km/h (331 mph)
Armament: two 20 mm cannons and two machine
guns plus bombs
Maximum altitude: 10,300 m (33,790 ft)

*anti-aircraft fire

Under US command

In September 1942, the RAF's Eagle Squadrons, manned by US pilots, are transferred to the US Army Air Forces (USAAF). They become the 4th Fighter Group of the 8th Air Force. All the pilots hand back their blue RAF uniforms and get olive USAAF uniforms. They continue to fly Spitfires until American Thunderbolt fighters arrive.

Mmm!

NOW YOU'RE UNDER US COMMAND, you eat US rations. It's great to have pancakes, burgers and cookies again.

I wouldn't like to be beneath this Thunderbolt!

Flying in a steel Jug

THE P-47 THUNDERBOLT is known by its pilots as the 'Jug'. Jug is short for 'Juggernaut', meaning an unstoppable force, because the Thunderbolt is such a big, heavy, powerful and strong aircraft. It is the biggest single-seat fighter of its day.

IT'S A SAD DAY when your Spitfire is taken back by the RAF because you'll no longer get to fly in one.

*So long, old friend... *sniff**

P-47D Thunderbolt

It's 'plane' to see she's quite a fighter!

Handy hint

Don't fire too soon – wait until your target is within the range of your guns.

P-47D THUNDERBOLT

Engine: 2,535 horsepower Pratt & Whitney R-2800
Wingspan: 12.4 m (40 ft 9 in)
Top speed: 697 km/h (433 mph)
Armament: 8 Browning machine guns plus bombs and rockets
Maximum altitude: 12,800 m (42,000 ft)

Congratulations, old boy!

ON YOUR LAST DAY under British command, you receive a medal to mark your service with one of the RAF's famous Eagle Squadrons.

31

Peace at last

Germany surrenders on 7 May 1945. The war in Europe is over, though the war in the Pacific will carry on for another three months. You are in London on leave when you hear the good news. You've survived and soon it will be time to go home to the USA! You join thousands upon thousands of people in front of Buckingham Palace, the official home of the British royal family. When the royal family and Prime Minister Winston Churchill come out onto the palace's balcony, the crowd goes wild. Lots of soldiers, sailors and airmen throw their hats into the air. One of them, a Wren (a member of the Women's Royal Naval Service) called Kitty Cardle, loses her hat. When she goes on duty without it the next day, her superiors charge her with being improperly dressed!*

The Wren, Kitty Cardle, is the author's mother.

I sure won't miss the brussels sprouts!

ABOVE: YOU'RE DELIGHTED to be back home, but you'll never forget the pilots who didn't make it back with you.

ONE OF THE FIRST THINGS you do is have a meal – steak and fries, and as much as you can eat. You're lucky, because food is still scarce back in Britain.

AT THE AIRFIELD where you learned to fly a biplane, a youngster admires your medals...

I'd like to be a pilot one day.

Glossary

Air fair A day or more of flying displays and competitions to entertain spectators.

Allies The countries that joined forces to fight against Germany, Italy and Japan, which were known as the Axis powers.

Altitude Height above sea level.

Biplane A plane with two main wings, one above the other.

Briefing A meeting held before a mission to give pilots their instructions.

Canopy The transparent cover over a plane's cockpit.

Cockpit The part of a plane where the pilot sits.

Drogue A small parachute or windsock towed behind a plane and used as a practice target by fighter pilots.

Eagle Squadrons The three RAF squadrons of American pilots.

Ferry pilots Pilots who delivered new planes to RAF squadrons during World War Two.

Fuselage The main body of an aircraft.

Going solo Flying a plane alone, without an instructor, for the first time.

Ground controllers A team of people who communicate with aircraft and keep track of their positions.

Ground crew The people who repair fighters and bombers, and keep them flying.

Gunnery practice Learning to use guns.

Kamikaze A Japanese word meaning 'divine wind'. It was the name for suicide attacks on Allied warships by Japanese pilots towards the end of the war.

Mission A military operation such as an air attack or bombing raid. A mission or attack by one aircraft is also called a sortie.

Morse code A method of sending messages as a series of long and short sounds or visual marks.

Nazi Party The political party that ruled Germany from 1933 to 1945; led by dictator Adolf Hitler, it tried to exterminate certain ethnic groups, especially Jews.

Newsreel A short film showing events in the news.

Night Witches A regiment of all-women pilots in the Soviet Air Forces during World War II.

Pesticides Chemicals which are sprayed over crops to eliminate pests.

Pylon One of the towers that mark out the course for an air race.

RAF The British Royal Air Force.

Ripcord The cord that, when pulled, releases a parachute.

Scramble To get a plane into the air as quickly as possible.

Stunt An aerobatic manoeuvre carried out by a pilot to impress or entertain spectators.

U-boat English term for a German submarine.

Undercarriage The wheels that support a plane while it is on the ground.

Wingspan The width of a plane from one wingtip to the other.

Wren A member of the Women's Royal Naval Service – the female branch of the British Royal Navy.

Index

Battle of Britain, 1940-1941

Hitler intended to invade Britain on 15th September, 1940. But without control of the skies, his armies couldn't cross the English channel in safety. Hitler wanted his airforce, the Luftwaffe, to wipe out the RAF before the invasion took place.

The Battle of Britain, which began on 10th July, 1940, was the first battle fought entirely in the air.

To begin with, Germany bombed British airfields and aircraft factories. Although this tactic might have secured a German victory, Hitler instead ordered his planes to begin bombing British cities in revenge for the RAF bombing of Berlin.

At first British cities were poorly protected, but by 1941 the RAF had radar-equipped planes, better searchlights and accurate anti-aircraft guns. The RAF also developed new tactics such as the 'Big Wing', in which hundreds of fighters joined forces to attack the incoming German bombers. British planes such as the Hurricane and the Spitfire could outfly many Luftwaffe bombers and fighters. The mounting casualties forced the Luftwaffe to switch to night raids, and it carried out its last mass raid on 15th September, 1940. Smaller raids continued until 16th May 1941 when they stopped completely. The Battle of Britain had been won by the British RAF.

Other World War Two vehicles

World War II wasn't only fought in aircraft: battle was also waged on land and at sea with a wide range of different, often groundbreaking, vehicles.

In the early part of the war, German submarines, or U-boats, caused enormous damage to allied merchant ships with their deck guns and torpedoes. Many seamen died terrible deaths, burnt in flaming ships, choking on oil or drowning in the Atlantic ocean. Often whole crews went down with the ship. During the period from January to August 1942 the Germans sank 609 American ships for the loss of only 22 U-boats.

Having first been used in World War I, tanks played a major role in World War II. The Allied forces and Germany experimented with building new and ever more fearsome types of tank. Germany built the gigantic Panzerkampfwagen VIII Maus tank, which weighed 180 tonnes. It had a gun big enough to blow any enemy tank apart at middle range. But it was so heavy that it couldn't safely cross most bridges and no engine could make it move faster than 13 kilometres per hour!

U-boat

Torpedo

Top World War Two pilots

Marmaduke Thomas St John Pattle was born in South Africa but travelled to Britain to join the RAF at the age of 20. Although records of his confirmed kill tally vary, he shot down at least 40 enemy planes and perhaps as many as 60 in only one year of service fighting in North Africa and Greece. By the time of his death, shot down in the Mediterranean in April 1941, he had become the top RAF fighter ace in World War Two and his record remained unbeaten.

German pilot Erich 'Bubi' Hartmann, however, was the highest scoring fighter pilot ace in both World War Two and the entire history of aerial warfare. He shot down a total of 352 Soviet and American aircraft in the war, taking to the skies at the age of only 20. So feared was he by his enemies that the Soviets took to calling him the Black Devil. After the war had ended, he became a flight instructor.

Chuck Yeager, an American World War Two fighter pilot, shot down many enemy aircraft but is best known today for being the first person to break the sound barrier. He did this whilst flying a Bell X-1 aircraft in 1947.